ENDORSEMENTS

"Bob Chancia's book *God's Red Carpet* is refreshingly different as a daily devotional guide. Here is the heartbeat of one who knows the streets of New York City with a burden to share biblical insights with those who live a fast-paced life. It is a book that will not only encourage and uplift but also will be read again and again. The reader will enjoy it…I know I did."

Dr. Donald R. Hubbard, Pastor Emeritus,
Calvary Baptist Church, New York City

"Here is a spiritual boost for those living life in the fast lane. *God's Red Carpet* comes out of the everyday experiences of a man who has walked in Christ's footprints through the push and shove of the advertising world. In Bob Chancia we have a man who is practicing what he's penned."

Jim Rose, Pastor Emeritus, Calvary Baptist Church,
New York City; Senior Pastor, Packsaddle Fellowship,
Kingsland, Texas.

"Bob Chancia has hit a homerun by combining a love for the Word of God with a profound understanding of our culture. *God's Red Carpet* will help you integrate faith in Christ with everyday life. Bob's sincerity and authenticity are real. This book will encourage you on your spiritual pilgrimage."

Pastor Cliffe Knechtle, Grace Community Church,
New Canaan, Connecticut

GOD'S
RED
CARPET

To Josh + Richele,
Walk with Christ, + realize
blessing forever !
Love,

Bob Chancia '08

BOB CHANCIA

GOD'S RED CARPET

TAKE A WALK WITH GOD AND NEVER SAY DIE!

Tate Publishing *& Enterprises*

Published by Tate Publishing & Enterprises, LLC
127 E. Trade Center Terrace | Mustang, Oklahoma 73064 USA
1.888.361.9473 | www.tatepublishing.com

Tate Publishing is committed to excellence in the publishing industry. The company reflects the philosophy established by the founders, based on Psalm 68:11,
"The Lord gave the word and great was the company of those who published it."

Book design copyright © 2008 by Tate Publishing, LLC. All rights reserved.
Cover design by Kellie Southerland
Interior design by Stephanie Woloszyn

Published in the United States of America

ISBN: 978-1-60604-140-6
1. Christian Living: Spiritual Growth: Spiritual Formation
2. Inspiration: Motivational: Devotional
08.06.01

DEDICATION

To the Creator of the universe who plucked me out of Utica, New York, and led me to the center of New York City in order to grab hold of me.

To my wife, Marian, and my parents, Florie and Allie, who surrounded me with so much love that I want to share God's unconditional love with you.

ACKNOWLEDGEMENTS

To the Sonlight Prayer Group that has met weekly in the upper room on 57th Street in Manhattan for over twenty years, which compelled me to stay in God's Word and be a discipler.

To Beverly Quinlan, my computer brain, who lovingly reviewed these chapters and submitted them with the technical expertise required.

To Dr. Roy and Patti Roberts who inspired me with their compassion and love for the hurting while serving in New York City.

To my twin brother, Dick, who made some important changes to this work with his careful editing.

CONTENTS

FOREWORD

I was taken aback when my brother asked me if I would write the foreword to his book. I have no degrees in theology or a single seminary credit. I know the forwards in basketball play on the baseline, nearest the basket, and await assists from the perimeter to score. In the military, "forward march" means to advance toward victory. Maybe he chose me because I am his identical twin brother and when it was time to exit the womb, I led the way forward to our new beginning.

In this twenty-first century, we are all on life's treadmill: working hard, striving to achieve, pressing on to survive, depending on futile human attempts to get somewhere. My brother felt led to help free us from some of this futility. He uses thirty-one pure and simple nuggets of truth, all easy to understand, to aid us in adding meaning to our lives. This time, he is leading me to a new understanding of this realm, as a time to prepare for forever! I hope you read on and move forward with us on God's red carpet.

Dick Chancia

PREFACE:
ESCAPADE IN WONDERLAND!

In the beginning God created the heavens and
the earth.

Genesis 1:1

There's no denyin' life is tough, but if you promise
to read on, I promise that this will be a red carpet
to wonderland for you. So, what's your life like right
now? Suppose that you had to give a State of the
Union address on your life and sum up in a status
report what's really going on with you. Would it
be positive or negative? Would it be light, dim, or
darkness? Would others be pleased and encouraged
or more importantly, how would *you* feel about you?
And, even most importantly, how would your creator
feel about this very unique and special person that's
been created, that's like no other person in all of
creation?

Hey, wait a sec, maybe I'm jumpin' ahead of myself.
Maybe you don't believe in a creator who is supreme
over all and you think that you're just the result of
some time/chance explosion. The fact of the matter
is that you do exist and somehow you did come into

being for whatever reason. You *do* have life and that's just a fact. You are unlike the plant and animal realm in that you can reason and have genuine emotions and concerns. You aren't mere matter and you really do matter! So what's this life that's all about you all about? Is it really all about you? Are you happy and content or could it be better? Are you just drifting along, taking one day at a time, crossing off the calendar days, and waiting for December?

I trust that this little book will give you renewed purpose and self-worth. After all, you are important, and there's no one else quite like you in all the universe. I have an identical twin brother, and we are probably as alike as two human beings can be. We have the same gene and chromosome make-up as we started out biologically as one egg that somehow split off into two equal parts. And even though we were reared by our parents and family to be almost like one, no matter what nurture provided to keep us alike, nature still has programmed our individuality. No two individuals are exact duplicates. We all have special qualities and temperaments that make us unique and special and quite like no one else, and that includes me and you. Rev. James O. Rose, noted Bible scholar and educator says, "Each and every one of us is God's *masterpiece.*"

So you are unique and special and have been given the gift of life. Well then what are you making of it? If you continue reading, I'm hopeful that you may discover some truths and answers that will give your life fresh meaning and maybe even a whole new purpose. Sometimes, all we need is a jump-start to get us going in a more satisfying direction. Maybe you're already satisfied with your life and I hope that you are. I still think that this easy read will encourage your heart and enlighten you to some new perspectives for a more fulfilling existence on this planet earth.

Would you just give it a try? It can serve as a month's journey by reading just one chapter a day or take it in at your own pace. It'll be like a little escapade in wonderland. Way better than Disneyland or Disneyworld. Because (I hope I don't scare you away now) it's about God. Even if you don't think that there is a God, read on anyway. And if you come away with a change of heart, you'll literally be on an escapade in wonderland because God is truly wonderful, and he wants to provide a way out of your troubles for you. He sincerely wants your life to be a *joyride!* Wanna go on a spiritual joyride? Then step out on to God's red carpet!

Bob Chancia
November 2007

1. THE GOOD NEWS QUIZ!

For *God* so loved the world that he gave his only begotten Son, that whoever believes in him should not perish but have everlasting life.

> John 3:16 (author's emphasis)

Did you notice that *immediately* here, it is *all about God?* Immediately we see that God is the one who gets everything started. He is the *initiator!* The verse says *for God…*

What is he the *initiator* of?

Answer: *Intimate, intense,* and perfect love. It doesn't say that God just loved. It says that he *so* loved.

Who does he love so very, very much?

Answer: The world, the whole world. His love is all *inclusive!* It includes everybody, *including you!* His love is not exclusive. It leaves no one out. He is not willing that anyone should perish.

His perfect and *all-inclusive love* is never without action. When someone loves someone, they *initiate* action. They get *involved!*

How does God get involved?

Answer: He gives something away for *free*. He gives much more than something; he gives *someone*—someone very precious to him. He gives away his only begotten Son for *free!* So He offers us the very best that he has. He doesn't hold anything back.

Who does He offer it to?

Answer: Anyone who will receive it. A gift is not a gift until we take it. Whoever believes in him will take it and that can include you. No one is left out. I told you that his love is *inclusive* and not exclusive.

So, what's in it for you?

Answer: *Everlasting life*—what more could we ask for? So his love is *infinite* too. Yes, it lasts *forever!* Do you want to live *forever* and ever, even after you die and leave this earth and live with God in heaven and with all of your loved ones who took the free gift? Then take his *free* gift *now!* Go ahead and ask him for it. He promised, before the beginning of time, a faith and knowledge resting on the hope of eternal life, and God doesn't lie! He's waiting to take you by the hand as his important guest and personally escort you on his grand and impressive red carpet of life.

I told you that it was all about him. He's the *one* who said, "*I am the way, the truth and the life*"!

For I am convinced that neither death nor life, neither angels nor demons, neither the present nor the future, nor any powers, neither height nor depth, nor anything else in all creation, will be able to separate us from the love of God that is in Christ Jesus our LORD.

Romans 8:38–39

2. MAPQUEST TO HEAVEN!

Jesus answered, "I AM the way and the truth and the life. No one comes to the Father except through me."

John 14:6

I AM is who He is. He is the great I AM! That is one of His great names. That's who Jesus is. Then *what* is he? He's a person of the highest degree. He has the ideal personality! He describes himself in the verse above. He says that he is the *way!* He's our directions, our pathway, our roadmap, and our compass toward righteousness. He's the *highway of holiness.* Jesus is the only one to guide and direct our steps because He's the only one who is holy. No one else is holy. Holy means to be set apart from all else or to be uniquely superior, perfect, and flawless in every aspect imaginable. As he chooses, he will begin to set us apart and purify us, which is a process that He works in us as we submit to His authority. So He becomes our only avenue or way to...*truth!*

He's the absolute unquestionable truth. He's perfectly honest, just, fair, and pure. Pure truth, that's what he is. He's the *hallmark of honesty.* There is not even one infinitesimal iota of untruth about him. Jesus is the genuine example of the purest of the pure. He's so pure that he exudes the highest quality of personhood that ever was or ever will be. And when we place our trust in him, He imparts who he is to us, and we get to share in his life. That's why he's our only hope of real *life!*

It's life now, because his spirit of life comes to dwell in us when we invite him to come in. And his spirit is living in us to pour out his life into our spirit and become one with us. Then his life that is in ours begins to flow out of us toward others that we encounter. And, because his life is eternal and his eternal life is now residing in us, our life becomes eternal in him who has paved the way for us by dying on the cross. Having paid the penalty for our blunders allows the Father in heaven to accept us as guiltless because the perfect, guiltless one paid our debt and we now share his guiltless perfection. He becomes our guilt offering. It's all because of him and what he did for us, so he becomes our only *hope of heaven.*

That's why we can't possibly come to the Father who is in heaven unless we go via his way, truth, and life. He loves us so much that he offers us such a beautiful pathway. But remember, that pathway goes through the cross and the cross leads all the way to

Glory! His shed blood is our red carpet to heaven! So just follow his roadmap and you'll never get lost again. It's the *only way to get there!* And there are no tolls. It's a freeway with EazyPass already paid for us. He's also your navigator, so don't forget to take him along for the ride. Think about it…God came all the way down from heaven, in the person of Jesus, just to open the way for us to get there!

But what about those people who never heard of Jesus, like some folks in primitive lands where a missionary has yet to visit or the mentally challenged who can't comprehend all the facts? Look, God is perfectly fair and just, and he will righteously and justly evaluate the lives of everyone, those that have heard his truth and those who haven't. We trust that judgment to our pure and just God. But he will hold those who have heard his gospel responsible for what they did with Jesus. Oh, we're so quick to judge others based on our frame of reference. Thank God that we aren't the final judges and he is! His ways are not our ways and his thoughts are not our thoughts so we leave that decision with him. He's that pure, and he's that holy![1]

> Here I am! I stand at the door and knock. If anyone hears my voice and opens the door, I will come in and eat with him, and he with me.

> Revelation 3:20

3. HEAVEN HELP US!

> In my Father's house are many rooms; if it were not so, I would have told you. I am going there to prepare *a place* for you. And if I go and prepare a place for you, I will come back and take you to be with me that you also may be where I am.

> John 14:2–3 (author's emphasis)

We often use that little phrase when we're desperate and in a trying situation. We need help or we need to be rescued. We associate heaven with God, and we're really crying out for his help. Usually when we're hemmed in by our circumstances, we have the natural instincts to seek a remedy from somewhere beyond us. So we yell, "*Heaven help us!*"

What is this place all about? Is it real? Do we believe it exists? Those verses in John 14 tell us clearly that it is a real place and worth yelling for. First of all, in verse 2, Christ is telling us a lot about heaven. (1) *It's a place!* That's right, heaven is a literal place. Jesus said so! He says, "It's the place where my Father dwells and because it's his house, it's also mine because I am one with him." He doesn't only dwell in our hearts when we invite him in, but he also dwells with the Father in heaven. And in his house, there are many rooms.

This is a mind-boggling residence that Jesus says really does exist or he would have told us otherwise. Christ is perfect and can't lie so we can be sure that heaven is a *place*. Jesus says that it's *a place* that he is getting ready for us! Rev. David Paul Epstein put it so eloquently by stating, "In the presence of God, there is room for everyone who comes to him."

Besides being a literal place, (2) *it's a promise!* He says, "I am preparing it for you." Because this mansion he is preparing has so many rooms, you can be sure that he is there right now getting one all set up just for you. You have a personal room in his mansion waiting for your arrival. You don't need a reservation number or even a plastic charge card, you just need to receive him into your heart and he'll get your room ready. Not only will he get it ready, but he promises to come back and personally escort you there. Everybody loves a personal chauffeur and escort. Well, you will have one and *that's a promise* from God!

(3) *Heaven is a person!* Jesus says, "I'm coming back to personally escort you there so that you will be where I am!" Jesus is the *great I AM*, so when we consider all the things about heaven, the one that stands out the most is the fact that heaven is *a person!*

Besides being a literal *place* and an absolute *promise,* it's a perfect loving *person.* Psalm 73:25 answers the question that it raises—whom have I in heaven but you? If heaven is all of those things and we're gonna be there because we've trusted the "Landlord," so are all of our brothers and sisters who have received and trusted him. We'll be reunited with those we love.

That's why this real *place,* containing all the *promises* of God is about *people* too. Real live people like you and me will have our own room in God's mansion and we'll live with him and each other forever. No more tears, no more pain, no more separation and no more death. That's why the Apostle Paul described heaven in Philippians 1:23 as an existence that's *better by far* than any we can imagine. It's far better to be where Jesus is! We've got a new address waiting for us and we don't need to worry about paying the rent or the state of the real estate market. It won't cost us a cent because it's already been paid for. Christ paid it all with his blood when he visited us on planet earth! Better reserve your room there *now!*

> Now the dwelling of God is with men, and he will live with them. They will be his people and *God himself* will be with them and be their God.
>
> Revelation 21:3 (author's emphasis)

4. GOD'S RED CARPET!

I tell you, use worldly wealth to gain *friends* for yourselves, so that when it is gone, you will be *welcomed* into eternal dwellings.

Luke 16:9 (author's emphasis)

Does the barrage of award shows on TV ever wear you down? If it's not the Oscars, it's the Emmys, Tonys, Obies, Golden Globes, or what have you. We humans need to constantly award each other with accolades and statuettes to applaud and recognize our accomplishments. Even more disturbing than the award presentations are the red carpets that precede them. The stars in their most glitzy get-up, strut their stuff to the glare of the paparazzi's flash bulbs looking for the most attention and press clippings. The red carpet gets even more hype than the awards themselves.

What does a red carpet symbolize? It's a *welcome mat!* Once while living in Detroit, I went with some friends to the Detroit airport to pick up another friend who was returning from a trip. We brought along a roll of red paper and some confetti, and as she stepped off the plane, we rolled out the red paper to welcome her home. God also has a red carpet waiting to greet those who trust in Him when they get to heaven.

That's what God is telling us through the pen of Dr. Luke in Luke 16:9. He's calling us to attention by saying: "I tell *you*." It's like we're on a ship and hearing the command come over the loud speaker, "*Now hear this!*" Important information is forthcoming!

The command is to use the provisions that God gives us here on earth to make friends for ourselves. If we meet folks who are hurting and we've been blessed with what they're lacking, we should reach out to them. That wealth doesn't have to be money, but if we recognize something that they need and we've got it, then we need to share it, even if it's just a listening ear, an encouraging pat on the shoulder or a cup of cold water. Because when the well runs dry and our time here is up, the ones that we have encouraged will roll out the red carpet and welcome us into heaven! That is, of course, if they get there before we do. Sounds like a great reason to make some new friends.

Not only will those folks be our welcome committee, but I will not be surprised if they're not also the *crowns* that God promised we would get for serving him while on earth. Why do I think that? Because of

what Paul says in 1 Thessalonians 2:19–20. He told
the Thessalonian believers that his hope and joy or
crowns that we will glorify God with in heaven will
be those folks that we served in Christ's power while
here on earth. After Paul asked, in verse 19, "What is
my crown?" he answered in verse 20, "*indeed it is you.*"
Then we will take those precious crowns and give
them right back to him where they rightly belong.

That makes all the sense in the world to me because the most valued possessions of Christ, after his
Father, are the believers that the Father promised to
him. You see, he cares the most about his Father and
then us, more than anything else. I never thought
that the crowns would be literal crowns like those
of reigning monarchs. So I would say that Luke 16:9
is (1) a wise command (I tell you); (2) a worthwhile
cause (use your worldly wealth to make friends); and
(3) a welcome committee. (They'll welcome us into
heaven.) How good is that?

On God's red carpet, you won't need a famous
celebrity escort either. Christ has promised to personally come and get you and escort you home. All
the flash bulbs by all the paparazzi in the world will
pale sadly compared to his majestic, supernatural
light. And no need for any designer creations as we'll
be decked out in his garments of righteousness. Who

needs Oscar de la Renta? And they won't cost us mega bucks. They've already been paid for with his blood. Now that's a red carpet! So how big is your welcome committee gonna be? You better go out there and make some new friends! They'll love rolling out his red carpet for you!

For what is our hope, our joy, or the *crown* in which we will glory in the presence of our LORD Jesus when he comes? *Is it not you? Indeed, you* are our glory and joy.

1 Thessalonians 2:19–20 (author's emphasis)

5. ON THE DEEP END!

> Call to me and I will answer you and tell you
> great and unsearchable things you do not know.
>
> Jeremiah 33:3

God likes to hear from us, but he also wants us to hear what he has to say. This is all about prayer, and prayer is a two-way street. Here God is inviting us to dialog with him. I'm sure of that because verse 2 of Jeremiah 33 clearly says: "This is what the LORD says, that he made and established heaven and earth." Read it for yourself. What he's saying here is that if we call on him, he's gonna give us the scoop or some very profound advice.

Prayer is not just us spouting off to God about everything that we want. The most important part of prayer is our listening to him. We think we know what we want, but he knows what we need. We need wisdom from him, light and understanding, and that's what he promises we'll get. He's saying here, "Forget about what you think you want. I want to let you in on the *deep stuff!* I want to tell you about the great things, the things that really matter." Those things are so deep you can never search them out and find them on your own. They'll never occur to you.

They're so beyond you and every other man or woman. They're unsearchable. There so unsearchable, they're just like God. They're wonderful! Did you know that the Prophet Isaiah refers to God as wonderful? That's right; he calls God our Wonderful Counselor. And that word wonderful in the original Hebrew language of the Old Testament means "incomprehensible." In other words, his name "Wonderful" that Isaiah calls him means that God can't be figured out. To coin a new word: he's "Non-Figuroutable"!

So stop trying to figure God out because you can't. Isaiah said that he's wonderful or "non-figuroutable." That's why he's God and we are not. But he's willing to share all this deep stuff about himself with us. He simply says: "Call on me and I'll answer you and I'll tell you the deep stuff you can't ever know otherwise." Do you want to know the deep stuff that makes God who he is, or put in simple language, what makes God tick? That will make your life worthwhile and understandable. If you do, just pick up the phone and dial him direct. I promise, you won't get any answering machines.

But before you waste your quarter, you better be

prepared to *listen!* Remember, I said the best part of prayer and the most rewarding part is the listening! So, even though we'll never figure God out until we get to heaven and see him face to face, we can find out right now why he's so wonderful. Just rap with him and hear it for yourself. He wants to speak to you personally from his word in the Bible. He won't take you *off* the deep end, just *on* a much deeper beginning!

> And he will be called Wonderful Counselor, Mighty God, Everlasting Father, Prince of Peace.

> Isaiah 9:66

6. SO WHO WROTE THE BIBLE?

> Above all, you *must* understand that *no* prophecy of Scripture came about by the prophet's own interpretation. For prophecy *never* had it's origin in the will of man, but men spoke *from God* as they *were carried along* by the Holy Spirit.
>
> 2 Peter 1:20–21 (author's emphasis)

People have debated that for ages. How can you believe the Bible? It was written by mere men. No, it was not! It's the Word of God! And the argument goes on and on. If men wrote it, why should I believe it, no matter what it says? Because it's the logos which means word, and the word was made flesh and dwelt among us. Christ is the logos or word, and the Greek word logos also means *meaning!* Christ is where we get our meaning 'cause *he is meaning!*

Our meaning is wrapped up in a person, and the Bible is *his story!* Whether we want to believe that or not, the Bible itself answers that question. But it still requires a teensy bit of faith, the size of only a mustard seed, to realize that. So the case is closed. We won't argue the point any further. The Bible speaks for itself in 2 Peter 1:20–21.

Here God says strongly, *above all*. Above everything else, you absolutely *must* get this: no scripture came about by men! He says that it *never* had its origin in any person's mind or ideas or intentions. Men only spoke or wrote down the facts that *came from God!* Well, how did they do that? They were *carried along* by the power of his spirit. Much of the time they didn't even understand what they were saying or recording. God's Spirit just pushed them through. That's what the Bible says! Do you believe that?

The logos is the meaning and that's God's Word and that's *Christ!* Do you want to find meaning in your life? Do you want to find the true meaning even in your circumstances that you may not like or always understand? Circumstances that even frustrate you at times. Then go to his word and he will give you meaning and also peace in the midst of your troubles. But you *must* take that first little step. And it's not even a giant step. It's a little "mustard seed" step. Just believe what 2 Peter 1:20–21 says about the Bible and then trust God who wrote it.

He only used a few faithful men who picked up their pens and took some dictation just like a secretary does from her boss. These mere men merely recorded the facts for us. Allow me to quote my pastor, David Epstein, who makes a most profitable point for us.

"We need to know God's word not just to know the word but in order to know the God who authored the word. God reveals himself through his word." As you continue in this reading, it is vital that you believe that God wrote the Bible and *not* mere men. God's Spirit wants to carry you along too. Go to your bookcase and dust off that sacred book of meaning for your life. He'll take you on a red carpet walk to wisdom. *Case closed!*

> In the beginning was the Word, and the Word was with God, and the Word was God. He was with God in the beginning.
>
> John 1:1–2

> For the word of God is living and active. Sharper than any double-edged sword, it penetrates even to dividing soul and spirit, joints and marrow; it judges the thoughts and attitudes of the heart.
>
> Hebrews 4:12

7. NO ABSENT-MINDED PROFESSOR!

> Although the LORD gives you the bread of adversity and the water of affliction, your teachers will be hidden no more; with your own eyes you will see them. Whether you turn to the right or to the left, your ears will hear a voice behind you, saying, "This is the way; walk in it."
>
> Isaiah 30:20–21

Some teachers are better than others. Everyone has had at least one favorite teacher. We label too many of them as absent minded. God doesn't give everyone the gift of teaching, but he's given everyone who trusts in him one perfect prof. who will never be absent, let alone absent minded. That *one* is Professor Holy Spirit!

In Isaiah 30:20b, he tells us that our teachers will be hidden no more and now we will most definitely recognize them. No matter which way we turn, we will hear the voice of the Holy Spirit right behind us giving us directions so we won't ever get lost.

Sometimes, Professor Holy Spirit has to shape us up or teach us with the tough lessons of trials and suffering. I like the way that Isaiah describes sufferings in verse 20. He says they are the *bread* of adversity and the *water* of affliction. He means that they really are our teachers who don't intend to harm us but want us to learn some valuable lessons in our life's journey. Why does he call adversity *bread* and affliction *water?* Again 'cause he doesn't mean to harm us but instead lead us to a healthy life.

Bread and *water* are names for Jesus. He's the *bread of life* and the *living water!* God wants to use these lessons to lead us back to him or back to a healthy life again. Remember that he is *life* and *never death.* Aren't you glad that Professor Holy Spirit is showing us how to really live? That's why he allows all kinds of suffering in our lives. It's to drive us right to Jesus, where we will find *life* and *not death.* He's not only the perfect professor, he's also the best doctor in the house. So this professor is never absent minded but instead, he's my favorite teacher! If I learn my lesson well, he won't keep me after school until I get it right. So get this lesson about *bread* and *water* down pat 'cause it's really about practical everyday baptism in the Holy Spirit. He wants to immerse us in his life. I hope you get an A in this class because it's about the *one* who promises everlasting *life!*

I have come that they may have life, and have it to the full.

John 10:10b

8. FILL'ER UP!

Do not get drunk on wine, which leads to debauchery. Instead, be filled with the Spirit.

Ephesians 5:18

This verse says don't overindulge on wine. It will lead to us running amok morally. When we overindulge in our appetites, we're setting ourselves up for dissipation. God's not talking here about just wine. He means anything that we do to satisfy our human lusts. Everything that we fill up on for our sensual pleasure is like participating in some kind of orgy. These orgies become just wasteful little escapades or dispersions into life's many trivial pursuits. God says, "Don't do it! Don't get drunk! Don't put anything before me."

If God really means that for our good, then he better offer an alternative for us. And he does! He doesn't really offer one, instead he *commands one!* He emphatically says *be!* That's the *command! Be!* Be what? *Be filled!* So this Godly command implies *capacity!* Exactly, *be filled!* Not one quarter filled, not just half filled or three quarters filled, but *filled,* filled to capacity! Filled so much that we can't hold anymore! Filled to the brim or overflowing. Isn't there always a feeling of security when driving your car with a full tank of gas?

I remember my first pastor, Dr. Joseph P. Macaulay, saying, "A brimful of obedience brings a brimful of blessing!" That's just cause and effect. We reap whatever we sow in life. So in this godly command, the Lord is saying *be filled to capacity!* And just like a car, we need to keep filling up our tanks. Our spiritual tanks empty out daily, too, and always need careful refilling.

What does he want us to be filled to capacity with? The verse says with *his spirit!* That's right, the *Holy Spirit.* The Bible teaches that the Holy Spirit of God is our Comforter, the One Jesus promised he would leave us with, when he went back to join his Father in Heaven. So we are commanded here to fill ourselves with *the comforter!* Do you want to be comfortable in the midst of whatever troubles or frustrations you're dealing with? Then, *be filled to capacity* with *the comforter!* You'll be much more than comfortable. You'll experience that divine supernatural *peace* from your creator, who'll liberally lavish it on you just when you need it the most. In the nick of time!

If you believe him and ask him to do that, you'll be amazed. When you're really hurting, this sense of peace will come upon you and you won't understand why you're not falling apart at the seams in the worst of circumstances. Or maybe you will understand, 'cause you will feel God's presence and sense his compassion. You'll be overwhelmed with his love because you drove yourself to him and cried out, *"Fill 'er up!"*

But in reality, God is the one who drove you to himself. So you need to fill up only on him! Start your morning by reading a verse or two with breakfast. Your day will feel like a walk on the red carpet.

O land, land, land, hear the word of the LORD!

Jeremiah 22:29

9. TRINITY: TRICK OR TRUTH?

The wrath of God is being revealed from heaven against all the godlessness and wickedness of men who suppress the truth by their wickedness, since *what may be known* about God is *plain* to them, because God made it *plain* to them. For since the creation of the world God's invisible qualities—his eternal power and divine nature (Godhead)—have been *clearly seen,* being *understood* from *what has been made,* so that men are without excuse.

Romans 1:18–20 (author's emphasis)

We have *no* excuse! God has made himself known to us. The Bible says he has spelled it out and made it *plain.* How has he made it *plain?* By the creation of the world! The verse says that his qualities that we can't see, his awesome power and even the *Godhead* are *clearly seen.* Not only *seen* but *understood.* How? From *what he has made.* So we have no alibi. Just go and look at a sunset or a rainbow or a waterfall or the ocean or a hurricane, etc.

For starters, let's look at the big picture. What did he make that will give us a *clear understanding* of him? How 'bout *the universe?* And what about *us?* He made *us,* too, the apple of his eye. Let's take the *universe.* What is it? Well *uni* means *one,* and *verse* comes from the Latin *veracity* which means *truth!* So the universe is *one truth.* It's absolutely true; it's an absolute *fact* of life! What makes up this *one truth?* Three components: (1) space, (2) matter, and (3) time. Wow! Three equal aspects that exist together. In fact, they always existed together. They are three co-eternal aspects of *one truth.* If one is removed, the whole truth falls apart. Besides being co-eternal, they're also co-equal. One aspect is just as important as the others. Leave one out, and the *one truth* can't exist!

So the *uni-verse* meets all the qualifications to be a *trinity,* three co-equal and co-eternal aspects. Not only that, but each individual aspect is also a *trinity.* *Space* is comprised of the three dimensions: length, width, and depth; so space is a trinity in and of itself. Everything we know of occupies space. *Matter* is also made of three parts, for that matter: motion, energy, and phenomenon. Motion and energy combine to present an observable presence that we can realize with our senses. Like an iceberg. We can observe it 'cause it takes on material form that we can witness, like a snowflake or even just a rubber ball. Or the pen I jotted down these thoughts with. That's the phenomenon—we can see, touch, and smell matter. Then of course there is *time:* (1) past or yesterday, (2) present or today, and (3) future or tomorrow. Out of the past comes the present and from the present comes the future. If we remove today, there can't be tomorrow nor could there have been a yesterday. Leave one out, and the one absolute true fact of time breaks down. So the one truth of the universe is a trinity similar to its creator.

Why wouldn't a triune God create a triune creation? The past or yesterday is like God the Son, who already came and died for our sins. We call that *justification.* And the present is like God the Holy Spirit, who's setting us apart in *sanctification.* And the future reminds me of God the Father, who will one day glorify us to be like him in *glorification.* So we have justification, sanctification and glorification hinted for us in the three facets that make up the one fact of time.

God made something else that is very dear to his heart. He made *us!* Guess what? We are also little knock-offs of the Trinity concept. What makes up men and women? (1) Body, (2) soul, and (3) spirit. The body is our flesh, which is material, so others can see us. By our acts of the flesh, others can tell what our character is like. Our soul is our intellect or mind that is driven or inspired by our spirit, which is our feelings or emotions. But guess what? That's not a good example of a type of trinity because one day the body will stay in the grave and be separate from the soul and spirit, which will exist forever. So the three components are *not* co-eternal. They won't always exist together! The better trinity for men and women is (1) soul, (2) spirit, and (3) personhood or personality. The action of the spirit on the soul causes another phenomenon that others can observe with their senses. By our behavior, they realize our personality, which is the manifestation or unique personhood that makes us who we are. Now these three aspects: (1) soul, (2) spirit, and (3) personality are co-equal and also co-eternal and better qualify as a type of trinity.

Isn't it amazing that our triune God left his footprints in his creation for us to understand him better? Makes sense to me, in fact, just look around. See if you can find some on your own. He's left little trinities all over his universe. Take an egg for example: shell, yoke, and whites. Remove one and you're left with a big splatter or just egg whites. These aren't by any means perfect trinities. They're just little hints from the *one and only perfect trinity!*

It's all very logical just like logic: Major premise—I'm a man. Minor premise—all men sin. Conclusion—*I am a sinner!* And so are you and we all need this *one true God* who came to planet earth in the person of Jesus to rescue us from the penalty of our sin and offer us everlasting *life!* He's the only *perfect truth* in the uni-veracity! Just receive him and become *one* with the *one truth!* His Spirit will live in yours and give you peace until you are perfected with the Father in heaven. And beware of the evil one who will imitate the *one true God.* Satan will imitate the Father, and the Antichrist will one day appear and copy the Son, and his false prophet will poorly impersonate the Holy Spirit. Don't be faked out![2]

Hear, O Israel: The LORD our God, the LORD is one.

Deuteronomy 6:4

10. HAT TRICK?

Two are better than one, because they have a
good return for their work: If one falls down, his
friend can help him up. But pity the man who
falls and has no one to help him up! Also, if two
lie down together, they will keep warm. But how
can one keep warm alone? Though one may be
overpowered, two can defend themselves. A cord
of three strands is not quickly broken.

Ecclesiastes 4:9–12

If a player in hockey or soccer scores three goals in a
game, it's called a hat trick. Or if a team wins three
championships in a row, it's a hat trick. So sports
adopted the term to refer to any three triumphs in
succession. There's a wonderful hat trick tucked away
in the Bible for us to enjoy too. Referring to our wonderful "three-in-one" God in that way is much too
irreverent because in no way is our God any kind of a
trick. God is the real deal as is Ecclesiastes 4:12. Let's
examine these comforting words of scripture.

Two are always better than one 'cause they're twice
as productive. They bear more fruit. And if one does
slip, the other is there to assist and pick up his or her

fallen partner. These are encouraging verses of what it means to have a genuine friendship or a committed mate in marriage. There is no one to help someone who is alone. Loneliness is a sad state, which is why God designed us to be relational. Being alone is a pity because there is no helper in a time of need.

When two lie down together, they keep warmer. This suggests the added protection and security there is in a loving marriage. It's also much more difficult to overpower two. There is strength in numbers and even just two will put up a better defense when threatened than just one.

Now here comes that "hat trick" in verse 12. Again, it's really not a hat trick at all 'cause it too is the real deal! "A cord of three strands is *not quickly broken.*" That's because God is in the picture. He's not only in the picture but he better be the main strand of the three. Maybe that's where the term "one accord" comes from. Ever try to break a cord of three strands? Oh you can break it, but not so easily. Even when we have God in the mix, if he's not our focus or the main strand in our friendships, they will weaken and experience some flimsy times. And even if God has allowed you to be single, no one has to be alone. Remember, God is our perfect friend, spouse, roommate, or whatever!

So let's make sure that God is our *main strand* with which the other two are meshed. Then we'll have one strong cord that is rooted into our triune God. This is not about a hat trick at all. It's simply about *the abiding life!*

Remain in me and I will remain in you. *No branch* can bear fruit by itself: It *must remain* in the vine.

John 15:4

11. FLOWER POWER!

> As long as the earth endures, seedtime and harvest, cold and heat, summer and winter, day and night will never cease.
>
> Genesis 8:22

Springtime proves that there is life after death. It's the evidence of new life springing out of death and the "great pattern" of all of life is obvious: death and then resurrection! We see God's promise of this in Genesis 8:22: "As long as the earth endures, seedtime and harvest, cold and heat, summer and winter, day and night will never cease." God is saying to us, "(1) *I am patient with you!* As long as the earth endures or while it remains, I am patient and will keep it going as long as I have to for your sake. I'm long suffering and not willing that anyone should perish." God has staying power for us, and he's not in any hurry.

Then he says, "(2) *I will provide for you!* I'll keep supplying you with what you need because I am the Great Provider. That is one of my names." There will be seedtime and harvest, cold and heat, summer and winter, day and night. God will provide for us because he is generous with his power and grace!

And finally he says, "(3) *I promise you this!* As long as I keep the earth going, all of this will never cease! That is some promise, especially for us who don't deserve it because we've gone our own way and disobeyed him. Then why does he promise all of this to us? Because he is a God of great power and wonderful grace! God is faithful and upholds all things by the power of his word. So be hopeful and confident and *trust him!* He provides for man and beast as long as the earth exists.

When we plant, there will be a harvest. That's even more important in our spiritual lives. Are the seeds of his truth producing fruit in your life? If the seeds of his truth don't take root in our hearts, we are cheating God and his creatures. We are here to nourish each other with spiritual enablement from the gifts that he has given to us. We must inspire and feed others toward God's spiritual harvest; seedtime to harvest! The beautiful flowers of springtime blossom, then they fade and die and their seeds fall, are scattered and buried, and new life springs forth. And the pattern of life continues. Death but then resurrection! *We can count on that!*

> But your dead will live; their bodies will rise.
> You, who dwell in the dust, wake up and shout

for joy. Your dew is like the dew of the morning:
the earth will give birth to her dead.

Isaiah 26:19

12. WHAT'S SO GOOD
ABOUT GOOD FRIDAY?

Jesus said, "Father, forgive them, for they do not
know what they are doing."

Luke 23:34a

Good Friday is good because it's all about goodness
and wonderful and marvelous love flowing from our
perfect creator who is offering his perfect love to us
who don't deserve it. There's nothing bad about that.
He's so good that he saved us who are so bad. And he
gave up his life and his relationship with his Father
and his Holy Spirit to do it. Look at the scene. Two
other men, both criminals, were also led out with him
to be executed. Jesus said, "Father, forgive them, for
they do not know what they are doing." Imagine, he's
being executed for doing nothing wrong, and while
a spear is piercing his body and his blood is freely
flowing out, he is asking his Father to forgive us. He's
rolling out the red carpet for us! What's so bad about
that?

Matthew's gospel account says that the two robbers who were crucified with him both heaped insults
on him. So did all the religious leaders and the people

who were watching and even the soldiers who were there. Suddenly, one of the robbers saw the light. He must have been so mesmerized by Christ's behavior on that cross and his willingness to forgive us that he realized his sinful condition and rebuked the other criminal. Then he said, "Jesus, remember me when you come into your kingdom." And Jesus answered, "I tell you the truth, *today* you will be with me in paradise." Is that good or is that not good? A dirty rotten scoundrel just like us in many ways is given a free ticket to heaven just because he recognized Jesus as Lord at the last minute of his life and asked Jesus to remember him.

We can do the same thing. We can never earn heaven or be good enough on our own. All of our best works will never cut it in heaven, 'cause heaven is a perfect place, only for perfect beings like God. But when we know that we are not good and only he is, and ask him to remember us, he gives us his goodness and perfection so we can enter on his coattails. Think about it, he takes our sins and mess ups and gives us his perfection in exchange. He gets our sins, and we get his righteousness. I think that's a pretty good deal. Don't think about it any longer; *just take it now while it's being offered.* It was offered on Good Friday and it's still being offered today. That's what's so good about Good Friday. It's so good for us that it should be called "Great Friday." We should yell out like our society does: "Thank God it's *Good Friday!*"

> For it is by grace you have been saved, through faith and this not from yourselves, it is the gift of God not by works, so that no one can boast.
>
> Ephesians 2:8–9

13. CHRIST BOUGHT US BACK!

In Christ we have redemption through his blood, the forgiveness of sins, in accordance with the riches of God's grace that he lavished on us with all wisdom and understanding.

Ephesians 1:7–8

Ephesians 1:7–8 clearly tells us that Christ bought us back! In fancier words than "he bought us back": *we have been redeemed* or he redeemed us.

The little prefix *re* in *redeemed* is derived from the Latin *re* which means to restore or recover. So it means not simply to buy, but to buy the same thing back or to *repurchase*. It's like going to a garage sale and finding something you once owned, so you buy it. But it's much deeper than that. *Buy back* implies that we originally belonged to God or we were his possessions in the first place, but somehow *we got lost!* And he bought us back!

We were in his heart before we were born and we were his. But we got lost and he found us and bought us back. The verse teaches that he did this through the blood of his son. And he wants to restore us for the purpose he had for us before the foundation of the world. He also forgives us with his grace that he lavishes on us.

Here's an illustration from my life. When I was five years old, my mom took me and my identical twin brother shopping to buy some badly needed clothes. Five-year-old boys don't like to shop for clothes. In the store while trying on the clothes, we spotted identical twin teddy bears. We insisted that she buy them. She explained that she only had money enough for the clothes we needed. Well, we threw a tantrum in the store and insisted on having the bears. She didn't have the budget for them but somehow managed to buy them.

The twin bears were a fixture in our house through high school. We called them "the teds." They were part of the family. On a trip home from college, we missed the bears in our bedroom and asked Mom where the teds were. She explained that they were badly worn and tattered so she tossed them out in the spring cleaning. We were overwhelmed with sadness and asked her, "How could you throw out the teds?" Who knows where they are now. *They're lost!*

Anyway, just last summer while on vacation in Vermont, my wife and I went into an old general store. Upstairs, sitting side by side on a little bench were two brown bears that were exactly like the teds, only brand new. I didn't even have to think about it. I grabbed the bears and paid for them at the counter. I had found the teds, only they weren't worn and tattered but restored and recovered. *I bought them back!* Or I *redeemed* them fifty years later 'cause they were once mine and I loved them and now I found them. They didn't find me, but I found them and repurchased them. Mom probably paid two dollars each for them in 1941, and that was stretching her budget.

That's what God did for us *in Christ. We got lost* all on our own. We went our own way and disobeyed and rebelled. We were also worn and tattered from sin and carousing. But God, in his mercy and perfect love, wooed us, searched for us, found us, and *bought us back!* And he made us brand new too. And he did it with the precious blood of his son. We are new creatures in Christ!

So, in view of that, how can you not be forgiving and fair to your fellow human beings? God loves them so much that he bought them back with the perfect blood of Christ, and he wants to forgive them and you too!

> When these things begin to take place, stand up and lift up your heads, because your redemption is drawing near.

> Luke 21:28

14. MY KIND OF FAST!

> Is not this the kind of fasting I have chosen: to
> loose the chains of injustice and untie the cords
> of the yoke, to set the oppressed free and break
> every yoke?
>
> Isaiah 58:6

God's kind of fasting is all about his compassion and
mercy and that is always more important than any
religious exercises we can ever do! In Isaiah 58 God
told the prophet Isaiah to remind his people that they
seem or appear to want to find God and that they
seem eager for God to come to them. Isaiah's people
told God that they fasted or gave up their meals and
God didn't even take notice of it.

God responded, "I know that you fasted but on
that very same day, you went about and bossed people
around and exploited them. You quarreled and fought
with each other. You can't just give up food and then
go and do as you please. That's not the kind of fast
that I want!

"This is the kind of fast that I want: Be honest
and fair with each other and give your helpers and
those under your authority *freedom!* Don't order them

around. Share your food and help the poor with what they need too. And, most importantly, don't refuse to help your own family members, if God has blessed you with an abundance of something that they may need. Family also includes those who belong to your local church fellowship.

"Then," God says, "your light will shine and people will see Christ who is in you." Then God will also *answer your prayers* and be there to help you. He will guide you and satisfy you and you will be known as a *repairer* and a *restorer, then the* LORD *will make you happy!* We all want to be happy, but imagine being known as a repairer and a restorer.

This may seem to you like a pretty hefty request from God. Can we do all of this by our own efforts and in our own power? Absolutely not, but we can ask *Christ* who is in us to release *his* power and let *his compassion* be expressed through us. God will then use us to show himself off to our hurting world. Time's running out. Let's try fasting the way God wants us to fast!

> What shall I bring to the LORD? Should I bring religious works? Will those please God? Here's what God wants from us: to act *justly* and to love *mercy* and to walk *humbly* with God.

> Micah 6:6 (author's emphasis)

15. HUMBLE PIE!

If my people, who are called by my name, will humble themselves and pray and seek my face and turn from their wicked ways, *then* will I hear from heaven and will forgive their sin and will heal their land.

2 Chronicles 7:14

Most of us love pie and everyone has a favorite. Does God have a favorite? Could it be apple, cherry, banana cream, or none of the above? The correct answer is none of the above. His favorite is not one of our favorites. He loves humble pie and that's too hard for us to digest.

God's first requirement from his children is to be humble! He loves our thanksgiving and prayers and wants us to confess our sin and repent by just agreeing with him about our condition. *But he demands our humility first!* Even before everything else, he says to his own, "*humble yourselves!*" Did you notice that he says, "if my people"? So he's talking here to his people *not* unbelievers. *And* the *if* sort of implies that we might not obey him 'cause that choice he leaves to us. Oh, *if* we would only listen to him and do what he says!

His first requirement is to be humble. The very first Beatitude in Matthew 5 is "Blessed are the poor in spirit, for theirs is the kingdom of heaven," and the second one says that those who mourn will be comforted, and the third says the meek will inherit the earth. Those first three Beatitudes are describing the person who is humble. God demands humility *first* and foremost from his children!

And to be humble means to come to him and admit our need and condition. Admit you are weak and broken and need fixing and that you can't fix yourself. Admit that you are self-centered and want to be in control. Admit that you like to sin and are rebellious. Tell him who you really are and that you desperately need him to fix you up. That's what he wants from us first. He wants us to be honest with ourselves and honest with him so that we can be honest with others too.

Then, he will activate our fleshly spirits to join with his spirit that is in us and begin to change us to become more like him. We can't *change us* but we can *exchange* our desires for his. Now he can start transforming us which is the *exchanged life*—his life for ours. That's why the Apostle Paul could say, "For me to live is Christ." In other words, Paul is saying that for me to *really live* is by *Christ* living in me. Paul also said to consider others with higher regard than ourselves. That's humility!

So God demands *humility first*, but we cannot be humble on our own. Humility is a *person* and that person is *Christ!* We have to look way beyond ourselves and way apart from us to him whose spirit lives with ours and ask him for *his* humility. Then and only then, can we treat others fairly and justly.

Second Chronicles 7:15 says, "Now my eyes will be open and my ears attentive to the prayers offered in this place." How about that for another reward? Besides feeding us a slice of humble pie, God will *answer our prayers!*

16. INVITATION TO DINNER!

… and she gave birth to her firstborn, a son. She wrapped him in cloths and *placed him in a manger*, because there was no room for them in the inn.

Luke 2:7 (author's emphasis)

This will be a sign to you. You will find a baby wrapped in cloths and *lying in a manger*.

Luke 2:12 (author's emphasis)

So they (the shepherds) hurried off and found Mary and Joseph, and the baby, who was *lying in a manger*.

Luke 2:16 (author's emphasis)

So I've mentioned three verses from this Christmas drama, and dramatic the story is! Luke tells us the story in the second chapter of the Gospel that he wrote as he was carried by the power of the Holy Spirit. In these verses, the Holy Spirit realizes the importance of telling us that the baby Jesus was placed or *lying in a manger* three times! Why was that fact so profound that he needed to mention it three times? Here's *some* insight on this.

First we need to understand the meaning of the word *manger*. The word in French is *mangeure* suggesting a feeding trough derived from the Latin word meaning to eat or chew. Many Italian mamas say, "*Mangia.*" In simple words, a manger is a box or trough that holds straw or hay, etc. for horses and livestock to eat from. Mangers were kept in stables, barns, or caves, which acted as structures where the animals could be sheltered while being fed or given drink. They were channels or vessels that held food and water. In New York City we have a chain of restaurants called "Pret A Manger."

Because there were no vacancies in the inns and fancy resorts of the day for the Savior of the world to be born, Mary and Joseph were led by God to find a barn or stable, most likely a cave where she was able to place her new born infant on the straw of the feed trough or manger. The elite of society who managed or occupied the fancy hotels were too busy making money or partying and totally indifferent to find some room for the Savior of the universe to be born. When the angel instructed shepherds in a nearby field where they would find their savior, they were told that he was *lying in a manger.*

It's also interesting that God chose to announce the birth of Jesus to shepherds first, who were the despised rejects and outcasts, considered on a par with the prostitutes of their society. As rough and tough as these carousing macho men were on the outside, God knew who the hurting hearts and hungry souls of the world really were (and are today). And knowing that underneath their tough exterior was an inner longing and need for meaning, he chose them and they immediately headed to find a feed lot or cave where the mangers would be. They wasted no time searching out the spas or watering holes of the rich and famous. They were familiar with feeding livestock, as they tended their own sheep and knew exactly where to look.

It makes all the sense in the world that God would allow his only begotten son to be born and placed in a manger, where animals came to eat and drink. This was a humble family without a place to stay and God wanted to visit us in humble surroundings and let the hungry hearts know first, feel comfortable, and come and be fed also. So the shepherds came and were they ever fed! They found the Bread of Life and the Living Water there lying in that manger. As lowly and dirty and smelly and humble as that abode was, it provided shelter for these humble parents and their newborn *King of kings and Lord of lords.*

In the Old Testament, God had long before clearly instructed the prophets Ezekiel and Jeremiah to eat his word, chew on it, feed on it, get filled on it, and only then go out and speak his word to their people. He gave them a diet of *scroll food.* It's not strange at all that God allowed our Savior to be *placed in a feed trough.* He's still inviting us today to also come to dinner and feed on the Bread of Life and drink his Living Water.

That's the gift of Christmas. The humble Savior, purposely placed in humble surroundings, inviting the humble of heart to come and eat and drink. It's no wonder that Bethlehem Judah means *house of bread and praise!* If you haven't done it yet, immediately RSVP that heavenly invitation. Then, just like those sinful forgiven shepherds, go off and praise God for what you're feeding on and offer him to your hungry friends and loved ones![3]

> And he said to me, "Son of man, eat what is before you, eat this scroll; then go and speak to the house of Israel." So I opened my mouth and he gave me the scroll to eat.
>
> Ezekiel 3:1–2

When your words came I ate them; they were my joy and my heart's delight.

Jeremiah 15:16

17. MIRACLE MAN!

Here is a boy with five small barley loaves and two small fish, but how far will they go among so many?

John 6:9

How far can a man go with just a little? With Jesus, a little goes a long, long way because he's the *miracle man!* And besides that, he's the Miracle God/Man. Check him out in: John 6:1–15, Matthew 14:13–21, Mark 6:30–44, and Luke 9:10–17.

Jesus is being mobbed here 'cause he's a *miracle worker!* Everybody sticks by a winner, and who doesn't want to get well? So Jesus withdrew from the mob by boat with his twelve close friends and followers. It was time for the Passover feast. When he saw the mob following him by foot, he felt sorry for them so he taught them many things and even healed their sick. The disciples suggested that he send the crowd away so they could go to nearby villages and find food and lodging. Is it fair to say that these twelve guys were literally out to lunch? But Jesus asked Philip, "Where can we buy enough bread to feed this crowd?" He knew what he was about to do but just wanted to see how much faith Philip had.

Philip answered, "Eight months' salary couldn't buy enough food to even give one bite to each one." But Andrew, another disciple, presented a *small boy* with a *small lunch* (five barley loaves and two small fish). The boy was little; the boy was hungry; he didn't have much other than what his mom provided for him, but he was willing to give it away. Andrew asked Jesus, "Can you feed this mob with this? How far will this go?"

Jesus said, "Sit the people down." He then took the small boy's five loaves, gave thanks to God for them, and his disciples passed out enough for everyone. Jesus did the same with the little boy's two fish. He fed 5,000 men plus the women and kids who were there. When they all were full, he told the disciples to collect the leftovers and make up twelve large doggie bags. When the crowd saw this miracle, they said, "Surely this is the Prophet who is coming into the world." Offering God's people whatever little we may have opens the door for God to bless us. When our lives become red carpets for others, God's life becomes a red carpet for us.

Here are seven things we can be sure of from this lesson:

1. Jesus cares about us and whatever we need.

2. Jesus loves the opportunities to teach us and feed us.

3. His friends, just like us, were more concerned with their next meal.

4. Jesus only asks us to bring to him whatever little we have that he's given us.

5. No matter how small we are or how little we have, God can do *big things* with it *if* we're willing to give it back to him.

6. Trust him with your life, no matter how unimportant you feel.

7. Then thank him for supplying you with more than enough to help others.

> Now to him who is able to do immeasurably more than all we ask or imagine, according to his power that is at work within us…
>
> Ephesians 3:20

18. NO MORE MOTHER-IN-LAW JOKES!

> But Ruth replied, "Don't urge me to leave you or
> to turn back from you. Where you go I will go,
> and where you stay I will stay. Your people will
> be my people and your God my God. Where you
> die I will die, and there I will be buried. May
> the LORD deal with me, be it ever so severely, if
> anything but death separates you and me."
>
> Ruth 1:16–17

There are so many jokes around about mothers-in-
law, probably because it's one of the world's most
trying relationships. Why is there such competition
amongst spouses and their mate's love for their
moms? I can't answer that fairly because I had the
blessing of a caring, understanding, and unselfish
mother-in-law. She always put our interests first and
was a pleasure and fun to be around.

But I'm pretty sure I know why God shared with
us this special relationship between a young Moabite
girl with her Jewish mother-in-law from Bethlehem.
He chose the mother-in-law/daughter-in-law relationship, which we have made into a difficult one, to
demonstrate to us that with him every relationship

can work beautifully and result in blessings for all. Ruth and Naomi turned out to be one special and rewarded pair.

After Naomi lost her own husband and two sons in the foreign land of Moab, she insisted that her two widowed daughters-in-law remain there while she returned home to Bethlehem. After all, these two young girls had their whole lives ahead of them and they needed to remain in their native land and find new husbands. And despite all of her insisting, Ruth clung to her mother-in-law, but Orpah decided to stay put. It's incredible how Ruth responded to Naomi's urging of her to stay in her country.

Ruth said, "Don't urge me to leave you. I won't turn back from you. I'm going to go where you go, and wherever you lodge, I will lodge there also. Not only are your people going to be mine too, but your God will also be my God!" Had Ruth not embraced Naomi's God, the only true and gracious God of Life, I don't believe she would have been capable of saying what she said. But having embraced Naomi's God, she was able to embrace Naomi, her mother-in-law. And she went on to say, "I will also die and be buried where you die and are buried." And it doesn't stop there. Ruth also said, "May the Lord deal with me ever so severely if anything but death separates us."

The amazingly astute Bible teacher Dr. Donald R. Hubbard said,

> Ruth made her choice, and that choice was a commitment to permanently leave behind her old life as she knew it. And she was willing to walk into a new life that she did not know but she would believe God for it. Away from the old and into the new! She made her decision that day!

This is amazing loyalty, especially coming from a daughter-in-law to a mother-in-law. If I was a marriage counselor, I'd insist that every couple I counsel study Ruth's remarks. And if they couldn't sincerely say the same words to their future mates, I'd suggest they wait and pray for an attitude like Ruth's. That's what marriage needs to be about. We need to have the best interests of the other party at heart. Marriage should never be about what I can get from it but instead what I can bring to it.

Hopefully we will bring to it such an unbreakable loyalty to our God first, that the same loyalty and commitment will spill over towards our mates. Read the entire book of Ruth and see how generously the Lord blessed Ruth and Naomi. Ruth, the Moabitess, was so fruitful and honored that she's even listed in Matthew's Gospel in the genealogy of Christ. God blessed Naomi and Ruth. Ruth met Boaz, Naomi's prominent and respected relative, in his grain field. For Boaz it was love at first sight and Ruth's mother-in-law sealed the deal by coaching Ruth on how to enhance the encounter. Ruth gets a husband and a son, and Naomi's new grandson Obed becomes the grandfather of King David in the direct line of Christ. When God is the architect of your efforts, no one can stop them! So before you think about saying, "I do," ask yourself if you can honestly say: "Wherever you go, I'm there!" That's no mother-in-law joke!

19. WHO DOES GOD SAY HE IS?

For this is what the high and lofty One says—he who lives forever, whose name is holy: "I live in a high and holy place, but also with him who is contrite and lowly in spirit, to revive the spirit of the lowly and to revive the heart of the contrite."

Isaiah 57:15

In this passage, God tells us exactly who he is. He spells it all out simply and clearly for us. For starters, he tells us that he is high and lofty. Way above and beyond us. His ways are not our ways and his thoughts are not our thoughts. He's so far up there in every capacity that he is beyond our comprehension. In a previous chapter, I stated that he is so wonderful that he is "non-figureoutable."

We keep trying to figure him out, but we can't because, as my pastor David Epstein always says, "He is God and we are not." That should make us sigh with relief and just rest in the faith that he gives us. God says that he is high and lofty, and those are his words and not mine.

He also says that he is One. He's the high and lofty

One. He's the One and only, the absolute personifi-
cation of perfection. He's three persons that make up
the unified, harmonious one God of all creation. He
goes on to say that he lives forever. He is *eternal* in
contrast to us being finite. He is infinite and always
existed and will always exist. If we put our trust in his
Son, who paid the price for our misdeeds, we too will
someday live forever with him. So he is one absolute
truth and he lives forever. Why not? He is the way,
the truth, and the life!

He goes on to say that he is also *holy!* Webster
defines that as consecrated and sacred, spiritually
perfect and untainted by evil, deserving deep respect,
awe, reverence, and adoration. And then God adds
that he also lives in a high and lofty place. Has to be
that heavenly place. So that's who God says that he
is! To sum it up in one word that we can all get a grip
on: God is *pure!* That's who and what he is: *pure!*

Webster says that purity is free from any adul-
terant or anything that taints, impairs, or infects.
Immeasurably purer than clear water and air. Webster
goes on and on…free from defects; perfect; faultless,
free from sin or guilt; blameless and chaste. Now
here comes one of the many mysterious paradoxes
in God's word. God says, "I am all of those things
and I most certainly do live in a high and holy place

befitting who I am...*But*...I also live with anyone who is contrite and lowly in spirit or anyone who is humble enough to admit their condition, own up to their failings, agree with me about them, and come to me for their only way of escape. In other words, he also lives with us, who have put our faith and trust in *him.* He came to us from that high and lofty place in the person of his Son, to suffer and die for our personal rebellions. So his spirit of life now dwells with our spirit and our bodies have become the dwelling places or temples for his Holy Spirit! Is that *amazing grace* or is that *amazing grace?*

And why do you suppose that this high and holy God would stoop to our level and come and live with and in us? Well, he doesn't leave us hanging. He comes right out and tells us why. So that he can revive our lowly spirits and revive our humble hearts. He wants to do a makeover on us and transform us to be more like him. He wants to give us a new heart. That's why, because he's not only pure but absolutely pure and profound *truth.* He's Emanuel, which means God is with us. That's who God says that he is, mere truth. It's that *simple.* Don't take my word for it, I didn't say it. *Trust only him!*

Still think that you've got it all together? God has

an answer for that too. He has no regard for those who think that they are wise. He's that pure!

"Where were you when I laid the earth's foundation? Tell me, if you understand."

Job 38:4

20. PERFORMANCE REVIEW WITH GOD!

"Come now, let us reason together," says the LORD. "Though your sins are like scarlet, they shall be as white as snow; though they are red as crimson, they shall be like wool. If you are willing and obedient, you will eat the best from the land; but if you resist and rebel, you will be devoured by the sword." For the mouth of the LORD has spoken.

Isaiah 1:18–20

If you've ever held a job, then you know what a performance review is all about. There you are face to face with your boss, getting his or her perceptions on your job performance. The results always affect your wages as a certain percentage of an increase is rewarded or not. Bosses in the business world can be cold hearted and unfair and sometimes take drastic action and award us with "the pink slip" or dismissal. You're fired!

Not so with God. In Isaiah 1, we find ourselves face to face in the office of the boss of the universe, getting our performance review. Unlike much of the business world, we have a very reasonable boss. It's mind-boggling here that the creator of the entire universe says to us, "Come now, let us reason together." Not only does he want to reason together with us, but he invites us to! He says, "Come now." We can conclude that our boss in heaven is *one reasonable boss*. Don't you wish that your earthly boss was that reasonable?

Not only is he reasonable with us, but he is also very *realistic* about our performance. We have worse than an unsatisfactory performance, but he also knows that we have an impossible job to do on our own. It's more than a tough job. We have a condition to deal with. It's a severe problem with self and rebellion, and it's so bad that God says it's not beet red but it's like scarlet. But as bad as we performed, he says, "Don't worry, I will make you as white as snow! I'm rewarding you with a clean slate." And he doesn't let up on us. He says we're also as red as crimson. It's no wonder we often utter the expression, "Guilty as sin"! Then he goes on to say, "Don't get rattled. Relax! I'll make you like wool." He wants us to be like sheep and follow after him.

Only we have to be *willing* and just do as we're told. Now we're getting a little restless. That's a tall order. How are we ever going to do that and please the boss? This job is our bread and butter. We need to put food on the table. And here we are getting a bad review. Quit worrying. You will eat the *best* from the land! He goes on to say if we resist him and continue to do it our way, some back-stabber will devour us and get our job. There's plenty of those in the so-called "real" world. Look, God's kingdom is the only real world and he's the only true, fair, and genuine boss!

He's *reasonable* and he's *realistic* and he's also *reliable* and very *rewarding*. He's the one who described our reward. White as snow and just like wool, and I didn't say that, he said it. Verse 20 says, "For the mouth of the Lord has spoken."

You may be saying, "No way can I do what he asks. I'm just not willing and up to it." Of course we're not. But he is and he'll give us his willingness! His willingness is wrapped up in a person and that person is Christ. When we know and trust Christ, his spirit lives with ours, and when we connect with that spirit, it nullifies ours and we get his willingness. That's why he says, "I know all about your condition and I don't expect you to change. Just exchange your spirit for mine that is in you and I'll give you much more than willingness. I'm going to give you a promotion, so you'll be where I am just because you got a great job review."

Hey, wait a sec. I thought the review was bad. No,

it wasn't! Read the verses over again, only this time slowly and see for yourself. These promises are from a *reasonable, realistic, reliable,* and *rewarding* God who wants to save us all from ourselves. When's my next review?

21. RUN FOR YOUR LIFE!

For the wages of sin is death, but the gift of God
is eternal life in Christ Jesus our LORD.

Romans 6:23

The society we live in is controlled and monitored by laws. Without a set of laws, there'd be total disorder and life as we know it would be utter chaos or *snafu!* God didn't mean for our earthly existence to be that way, so he gave us a set of laws called the Ten Commandments to set some standards of morality. The children of Israel quickly learned that they were unable to keep those commandments as the drives of their flesh were too strong. So God in his mercy, hating all the law-breaking that was going on, visited us in the flesh, in the person of Jesus, to give us a new and better law. Jesus eradicated the old set of laws that we couldn't keep anyway, and he personally suffered and died for all of our mistakes.

Now, we just need to receive his payment for our mistakes and we are set free by the new and better law that he offers us: *himself!* The above verse is awesome because it contains the entire law of nature as well as the better and perfect law of God. I understand the law of nature kind of like this. (1) *We reap what we sow* in life. (2) *Selfishness self-destructs.* (3) *We are not islands.*

First off, whatever we invest in, we realize the results of, whether good or bad. There are natural consequences for all of our actions. Secondly, being completely obsessed with ourselves and feeding all of our appetites first, with no regard for others, will cause us to dissipate, become weak, and eventually die. And thirdly, we are not alone on this planet. Whatever we do will affect those around us and especially our loved ones. They will either rejoice with us or be terribly hurt by our behavior.

So clearly, the results of our bad behavior will be destructive like the verse initially states: "The wages of sin is death." That's the law of the land. Everything is gradually eroding. Science does not refute that. The Second Law of Thermodynamics is a universal law of decay. Material things are not eternal, and everything ultimately disintegrates over time, ages, wears out, and returns to dust. Death is the final manifestation of this law. It's simply cause and effect. We will reap whatever we sow. But God doesn't leave us there. With just that law of nature in operation, we would have absolutely *no hope!* Praise God that he didn't stop there. The verse ends up with the far better law or the law of God. "But the gift of God is eternal life. So everlasting life is a free gift from God, and it is through the suffering of his son who bore our sin on a cross to get us off the hook. He personally endured the pain and we get the gain. *No pain, no gain!* And you better believe that there was pain. It was pain and bloodshed that went through the suffering and death of crucifixion. This completely satisfied God as due payment for the sins of all of mankind. So just trust the One who took your sin to the cross and that will set you free!

That is the law of all of life in one short verse. The results of our willful behavior produce death, but the free gift of God's suffering son gives us everlasting *life!* I'm glad that God didn't cut us off with just the law of nature. Without that greater law of God at the end of the verse, we are *doomed!* But we're not because he offers us the gift of himself, wrapped up in his Son. You better take it and unwrap it and run to him for your life. It'll be a good run!

> Therefore, there is now no condemnation for those who are in Christ Jesus, because through Christ Jesus the law of the Spirit of life set me free from the law of sin and death.
>
> Romans 8:1–2

22. WHAT'S GOD UP TO?

For the eyes of the LORD range throughout the
earth to strengthen those whose hearts are fully
committed to him.

2 Chronicles 16:9

Do you ever wonder what God is doing right now
as you're reading these words? Is he involved in our
lives? Does he care what we're up to as we are asking
what he's up to? Is he just allowing the laws of nature
to run their course? He put those laws in place and
most definitely supersedes them. He can intervene
at his desire and interrupt any course of nature. The
law of God is supreme and our Lord still reigns over
his universe and can burst through with a miracle
whenever he likes. Our sovereign God, in his three
and one totality and majesty, is still King of kings and
Lord of lords.

That's what makes us conger up those thoughts
that God is way out there in the beyond and out of
our reach and imagination. And he most certainly is,
as 2 Chronicles 16:9 suggests. So we raise the ques-
tions: What's God up to? Does he really care about

me and what I care about? The beautiful paradox here, and the truth about the many other paradoxes about him, is that even though he's way up there, he's also way down here too. He dwells in every heart that has personally received his offer of everlasting life and that life is only in his Son!

And even right now, while his Spirit resides in my spirit, the verse says that his eyes, acting like a supersonic supernatural telescope, with a range spanning the entire earth and universe, are peering and searching for those hearts that are not just committed but *fully committed* to him. That's exactly what our God is doing right now. He's scoping us out and checking to see how committed we are. I would guess that he is disappointed because, if I am really honest with myself, I'll admit that I am not as committed as I need to be.

When he looks at your heart, what does he see? Proverbs 16:1 says: "To man belong the plans of the heart…" What are your plans? Verse 5 says, "The LORD detests all the proud of heart," and verse 9 continues, "in his heart a man plans his course, but the LORD determines his steps." Yes, he's not only in charge of our plans but also every step we take, in spite of what we may think.

Praise God that his peering eyes, ranging

throughout the earth, are filled with unconditional love and grace. He wants to give us a new heart. He wants to replace our hearts of stone with his heart of love and mercy. Receive that new heart now if you haven't already and rejoice that when his eyes land on you, he'll do exactly what he promised he'd do in 2 Chronicles 16:9. He'll recognize that new heart in a flash and he'll *strengthen it* just like he said he would. That's what our God is up to right this very moment. He's strengthening hearts that are fully committed to him. That's his business! So what are you up to?

"My son [my daughter], give me your heart" (Proverbs 23:26).

> I will give you a new heart and put a new spirit in you; I will remove from you your heart of stone and give you a heart of flesh.
>
> Ezekiel 36:26

23. NOTHING'S FOREVER EXCEPT FOREVER!

The world and its desires pass away, but the man who does the will of God lives *forever*.

John 2:17

There's a common expression in our society that says, "Nothing's forever." It's an absolute given that every one of us will pass from this world and what comes next is up for grabs. Some adhere to a life after death and some do not. Many believe that when we exit planet earth, we just fade away into non-being, like we were before our physical birth. The Bible doesn't teach a non-being condition. According to God's word and promises, we will all exist forever. Either forever with him in a perfect realm or forever apart from him.

Just the fact that we can be sure of physical death one day should make us ponder these thoughts. What do you think? Do you think it's all over at the graveyard? Or do you believe that your soul and spirit will continue to *exist* apart from your flesh and go on to live forever somewhere? God's word says, those who have received Christ's suffering and death as due payment for their personal rebellion will be absent from their bodies but present with the Lord in a split second at physical death. This is what we mean by eternal *life!* And the Christ rejecters will realize the result of their personal choice not to believe him and they will experience eternal *existence!* Either way, we don't cease to exist at physical death. It's a forever proposition whichever way you choose.

The above verse also claims that this world, with all of its hopes and dreams and plans *will pass away!* This we can't deny because we see it happen to people every day including those very dear to us. Besides that, God says so and he can't lie! The verse concludes that the one who does the will of God will *live* forever. Doing the will of God is trusting and receiving his Son. Living forever means to be in God's presence with all of the other folks who trusted Christ. The other option is just *existing* forever apart from God. What are you opting for? *Living* forever or *existing* forever? There's a tremendous difference. When we live forever, our minds, memories, emotions, and consciousness never cease. They are what make up our soul and spirit, and they leave our physical bodies and are immediately present with God in an everlasting state of perfected life.

Otherwise, our soul and spirit still exist apart

from our body, which leave the body dead. They also go on to exist in an eternal realm apart from our maker, without his love and light. We get to choose either state 'cause God gives us a free will. He doesn't force anyone to be with him who doesn't want to be. And God says the only things that will *not* pass away are his word and people. If we opt to trust his word, one day he will give us a new body to join with our eternal soul and spirit so we can experience eternity with him complete with body, soul, and spirit.

So your choice is an important one. It affects *forever!* You can forget about that common old expression that "Nothing's forever." Yes, nothing in this world is forever *except forever!* When we come to a fork in the road, we opt for one way or the other. Either way there are consequences. When we come to that forever in our journey, we better take the one marked *life* and not merely *existence.* Have a blessed journey! (More about this in the next chapter.)

> But our citizenship is in heaven. And we eagerly await a Savior from there, the LORD Jesus Christ, who by the power that enables him to bring everything under his control, will transform our lowly bodies so that they will be like his glorious body.
>
> Philippians 3:20–21

24. GET READY FOR LIFT OFF!

> For since death came through a man, the resurrection of the dead comes also through a man. For as in Adam all die, so in Christ all will be made *alive*.
>
> 1 Corinthians 15: 21–22

Who wants to die? If I were a gambling man, I'd wager to say that most of us would try to avoid death at all costs. And to be honest, it's downright scary for many of us. Why? Because there's too much uncertainty about it. But it's a natural fact of life and we can't avoid it. The Bible says there's a time to be born and a time to die. One day we will all exit Planet Earth. That's what is meant by dying. We die to this realm, but we don't really die! The fact of the matter is that you and I don't have to really die. We can continue to live forever and ever and ever. Life is that amazing! There's just no end to it! We can all be translated to a far better and eternal realm, just for the asking, in a twinkling of an eye or in an instant. I don't know about you, but I ain't dyin'!

Let me try to explain what literally happens at physical death and remove the scary uncertainties.

Are you ready for a joyride? Then get ready for *lift off!* Here's what really happens. When your vital signs finally quit and you stop breathing, you're proclaimed as medically and physically dead. And you are! *But*…that doesn't really mean dead. Dead to this realm, yes, but remember God has promised that we all will exist forever somewhere. Either with him or without him, whatever the case, we go on.

Here's what takes place at the instant of physical death, if we've trusted God's Son for his free gift of life to us. Our soul and spirit will *lift off* of our fleshly body in a split second and join the Lord in the spiritual realm, which is timeless and eternal. Life has not ceased because our soul and spirit make up the true essence of who we are as persons. Our soul and spirit comprise our mind, emotions, intellect, will, memory, consciousness, nature, etc. That's all the good stuff that makes us persons with personhood. Having a body does not qualify us as persons. The animal kingdom possesses bodies, and they aren't persons. The Holy Spirit of God is a person without having a body. Our personhood will never die but continue forever. At the precise moment of physical or clinical death, we will not lose consciousness or that unique personality that we all have. We're simply translated to another realm.

And at that moment of physical death, we will be very much aware of moving from this realm to the next one. That move can be a move to a far better realm for you and me. But if we don't *lift off* and join God, then we're instantly transferred with all of our personhood to a realm without God. So the lift off is key! When our soul and spirit are lifted from our body, the body remains behind. It's merely a casing or envelope that held everything together for our time here on earth. Our present bodies are designed to withstand the atmospheric conditions of this realm. But at physical death, the body remains here as our remains. Without the soul and spirit, it is very dead indeed. That's why if you touch a corpse it will never react or breathe again. Everything that was life in it has departed and the unique personality is no longer here. With personhood gone, the body remains lifeless.

We mourn at funerals and gravesites, but the person that we knew has departed and only the dead casing remains. At some future point God will gather up or resurrect our earthly remains, wherever they are or whatever condition they are in and make them glorious bodies suited for the eternal realm. He will join them with our souls and spirits so we will be complete with body, soul, and spirit for our forever life. We will be recognizable to each other

but in a perfected state. How he's gonna do that, I
don't know, but as my pastor Dave always says, "It's
just another day at the office for the Creator of the
universe." Nothing is impossible for him, and that is
part of the future plan he has for us.

God has promised us a perfect, joy-filled life with
him forever. Trust him for that! That's the only life
worth living for and nothing less. So you don't have
to really die. You can continue living from this day
forth into foreverland. God charted this course for
us, and he became like us in the person of Christ
for a short season (thirty-three and a half years)
to experience suffering and physical death. He has
demonstrated how to endure suffering and destroy
death. He conquered it and rose above it and wants
to do the same for you and me.

So we must accept his offer and receive his gift
of forgiveness. His voluntary suffering, death, and
shed blood erase all of our selfish deeds and become
our red carpet ride to paradise! Cash in now on his
completed work. It buys you a free ticket to forever!
You don't need to work for it 'cause he's already paid
in full for you! Are you ready for *lift off*? Then let the
free ride begin! The fulfilled life starts right now.

He has made everything beautiful in its time. He
has set *eternity* in the hearts of men...Ecclesiastes
3:11

25. GUARD DUTY!

If you make the Most High your dwelling—even the LORD, who is my refuge—then no harm will befall you, no disaster will come near your tent. For he will *command* his angels concerning *you* to guard you in all your ways; they will lift you up in their hands, so that you will not strike your foot against a stone.

Psalm 91:9–12

I remember pulling guard duty in the army. I dreaded it 'cause it was a big responsibility. I never felt strong and secure enough to keep watch over so many men. Much of the time, most of us would admit to feeling vulnerable and intimidated by the forces around us. It's no wonder that we invest in expensive insurance policies to protect our rights. The rich and famous even employ personal bodyguards, and presidents have the Secret Service to provide for their safety.

When I was a kid, I was always being reminded of my guardian angel that watched over me. Is that really true? Does each one of us actually have a special agent of God watching over us at all times? And if we do, why do bad things happen to us sometimes?

When we know God in a very personal and intimate way, through his Son, who suffered and died for our mess-ups, it gets even better than that! God doesn't promise just one special angel to protect us. He sends out a whole fleet of them! In fact, he commands his legion or host of angels to do the job.

Check out those four verses above carefully and see for yourself. Verse 9 says that if we make God our dwelling place, then no harm will come our way. We usually nullify that promise 'cause more times than not we don't abide that close to him. He's always there for us, but we've gone and left him. He's there, but where are we? We're usually off doing our own thing so that promise goes out the window. The promise is still there, but we are not. So whose fault is that?

But when we are there, abiding real close and comfy, really tuned into God, he says he'll order his entire squadron of angels—that's in the plural and not just one—to specifically protect us and all of our steps. He even goes on to say that these angels will go so far as to literally pick us up with their hands so that we won't be able to stumble on anything. That's pretty awesome protection. God wants to be our protection, but we just won't let him be.

Let me quickly share five personal incidents where God's squadron of angels surrounded me: (1)

When driving on I-95 south to Miami for my first day on a new job, the balding tires of my car skidded on a slick pavement and spun me out of control, landing the car on the shoulder facing north. A trooper came, got me turned around, and back on the expressway shaken but unharmed. (2) Friends and I were letting pre-hurricane/warning waves toss us around in the ocean surf in Florida, when suddenly I lost my bearings and was thrown to a piling, which I was able somehow to bear-hug. I waded out of that dangerous surf cut by the piling's barnicles. (3) With a borrowed dirt bike from an eight-year-old, I raced another eight-year-old on a gravel Vermont country road and was thrown over the handle bars, hitting the pavement chest first. Lots of bruised ribs and aches but nothing broken. (4) After asking a bus driver directions, who was stopped in the middle lane on Madison Avenue in NYC, I walked backwards to the curb only to be hit and thrown by a car coming in the first lane. I was flung in the air and landed on my feet unscathed. (5) While driving on Route 103 in Vermont with the right of way in a fifty-mile-per-hour zone and four passengers in my car, another car jumped a stop sign and smacked us broadside. I had the air-bag experience which engulfed me in safety. The car was totaled and my wife fractured her wrist.

In all five cases, God's legion of angels took the brunt of the blows.

In fact, Psalm 91 is all about security and protection offered by God to his children. Go ahead and read the whole Psalm and see exactly what's being offered to you. But keep in mind that this Psalm is conditional; like all of God's promises, it's cause and effect. We reap what we sow in this life. If we dwell or make our habitation in the shelter and protective shield of God, we will be at peace and rest in his shadow. But that takes staying real close to him at all times. You have to be pretty close to stand in someone's shadow.

So go ahead and reap the benefits. Try standing in God's shadow. Oh, we'll get distracted more often than not, and the world will pull us in its own direction as long as we're in this fleshly realm. But all we need to do is ask him to help us get in his shadow and stay there. It's much better than standing under a big golf umbrella in a sudden cloud burst. That's what prayer, Bible study, and hangin' out with other true believers are all about. They're about trusting God to do it for them!

Go ahead and give it a try. He promises you his support. That sure beats pulling guard duty!

He who dwells in the shelter of the Most High
will rest in the shadow of the Almighty.

Psalm 91:1

26. DADDY, DO IT!

A certain man from Cyrene, Simon, the father of Alexander and Rufus, was passing by on his way in from the country, and they forced him to carry the cross. They brought Jesus to the place called Golgotha (which means the Place of the Skull). Then they offered him wine mixed with myrrh, but he did not take it. And they crucified him.

Mark 15:21–24

Have you ever suffered so badly that you felt like you reached your limit and just wanted to give up? Then that's exactly what you need to do—*give it up!* When my nephew Alex was a little shaver and he couldn't do something on his own, he would cry out, "Daddy, do it!"—a sincere form of dependence and trust. When you can't bear up any longer, welcome to the club. Even Jesus has been there and done that in his fleshly days. He endured his cross in the limitations of his manhood and God provided for him and came to his rescue. He ultimately released Christ from the agony of the cross and then raised him from the dead. The Father came to the Son's rescue exactly when he needed him to. And he'll do it for us too. That's what the above verses are all about.

They should encourage us when we're in what feels like a humanly impossible situation. Because all of these humanly impossible situations are just that—humanly impossible situations. But remember, nothing is impossible with God. He did it for Jesus. Usually, the victim carried his own crossbeam. But when Jesus got too weak to carry it and it got too heavy and became unbearable, what did God do? He provided a *certain man,* who just happened to be passing by. Just happened to be passing by? I don't think so. This was a handpicked individual supplied by God, prepared, and available for a certain task—a certain man for a certain task. That's not coincidence. That's providential circumstance ordained by God for the specific task of *cross carrying.*

When God hands you a cross and it gets so heavy that it's way beyond you, go ahead and tell him about it. Admit to him that you're completely spent and this is out of your league. Tell him, "God, I want to carry it, I'm willing but I can't. *Daddy, do it!* I need you to take up the load." Offer it right back to him. He wants us to admit our ineptness and totally rely on him. Ask him, "Father, take it up for me because I can't do this on my own. *Daddy, do it!*" He did it for Jesus. He provided a certain man.

He's got a certain man all ready for us too. This certain man is very experienced in cross carrying. He's had some real on the job training. Jesus will gladly help carry your cross if you'll just ask him to. He told us that his burden is light and that his yoke is easy. So don't try to carry your crosses alone. If he gives you the willingness, he'll give you the strength. But remember, it will be his willingness and his strength imparted to you. He loves it when we ask him to be our supply. That's what worship is all about. Admitting who we aren't and who God is, then trusting and desiring him to bail us out.

He already did that on that Place of the Skull, and he wants to keep doing it for those who ask him to. Need rest? Then ask him. *Just do it!* And your Daddy in heaven will!

> Come to me, all you who are weary and burdened, and I will give you rest. Take my yoke upon you and learn from me, for I am gentle and humble in heart, and you will find rest for your souls. For my yoke is easy and my burden is light.
>
> Matthew 11:28–30

27. WILL IT FLOAT?

The man of God asked, "Where did it fall?"
When he showed him the place, Elisha cut a
stick and threw it there, and made the iron float.
"Lift it out," he said. Then the man reached out
his hand and took it.

2 Kings 6:6–7

The Prophet Elisha's men were down by the Jordan
River cutting down trees to build a bigger place for
them to meet. But first one of the men urged their
leader to accompany them there and he graciously
complied. This wise one was well aware of the power
of Elisha's presence and the impact it would have on
their efforts. One of the men was cutting down a tree,
and suddenly his iron ax-head came loose and it fell
into the water. "Oh, my lord," he cried out, "it was
borrowed!" Have you ever been in a predicament like
that? Someone had let you borrow something that
you needed for a specific task and a mishap occurred
and the item you borrowed got lost, broken, or badly
damaged? A sense of panic overcomes you, and you're
totally lost for a solution. Those are the times that we
all need to be delivered.

As soon as this panicky woodcutter cried out, his master asked, "Where did it fall?" Thank God that one of those men knew in advance that they would need their master to tag along. Do you rely on God's presence in all of your experiences? You should! And not just in the bad times either but also in the good ones. Jesus promised *never* to leave us or forsake us. We can never anticipate when a tough situation will occur. This man had a *problem,* but he knew exactly where to turn. Not only did he have a problem, but fortunately for him, he had a major *presence.* That man of God, the Prophet Elisha was in their midst.

This man of God asked his servant where the iron ax-head fell. When the exact place was pointed out, Elisha cut a stick and threw it where the mishap occurred. That reminds me of another very significant stick, the wooden crossbars that Jesus was nailed to on that hill of Golgotha. Jesus has made it his prime mission to find and rescue the lost. Immediately that sunken ax-head came to the surface of the water. Will a heavy iron ax-head made to cut down trees float? Not naturally, but when God's on the scene, it'll float! Understand that God put those laws of nature in place and if he chooses, he can rearrange their natural course. Having God beside us in this natural realm is having access to the supernatural in charge of the natural. David Roper, in his book *Out of the Ordinary,* says that this was indeed a miracle 'cause "Elisha caused the ax-head to 'flow' as the Hebrew text says. The ax-head was set in motion by a sudden rush of the water so that it drifted out of the deep water and into the shallows where he could retrieve it."

I don't know about you, but that makes me feel very secure. *Will it float?* Of course it will, if God wants it to. Not only did this troubled woodcutter have a problem and a presence, but he now had a provider. "Lift it out," the man of God said. And the woodcutter reached out his hand and took it. This woodsman suddenly realized one more thing. Besides having a problem and a presence and a provider, he also had at his disposal the great promise of God. If we too would only reach out and receive what God has provided for us, we also will be delivered. This is a wonderful picture of resurrection power in the Old Testament. Jesus had sunk to an all-time low on that stick, he was buried and spent three days in hell but then miraculously rose again, defying all of the laws of nature that he himself had put in place.

Another gifted pastor friend of mine, Dr. Donald R. Hubbard, once said, "Plunge the cross of Christ into your problem area and find God's resurrection power." *Will it float?* Most decidedly, but we must reach out and take what's being offered. Jesus is a free love gift from the Father. Go ahead and take him for all he's worth. He's worth it all!

> Jesus said to her, "I am the resurrection and the life. He who believes in me will live, even though he dies; and whoever lives and believes in me will never die. Do you believe this?"
>
> John 11:25–26

28. WHAT, ME WORRY?

> Do not be anxious about *anything,* but in *every-thing,* by prayer and petition, with thanksgiving, present your requests to God. And the peace of God, which transcends all understanding, will guard your hearts and your minds in Christ Jesus.
>
> Philippians 4:6–7

Don't you worry! That's what God says! Yeah, *but…* there's always something that's nagging my heart and I just can't shake it off. Most of the times we have to admit we are big time worriers. Forget about those something kinds of things. God says not to worry about *anything!* When you look back at your life in the rear view mirror, doesn't it amaze you that the things you worried about didn't happen but other things that you never anticipated did occur? One ounce of worry will not change God's plans for our lives one iota. What he wills will always take place right on time in spite of us. And whatever he allows will always be what we need for him to direct us where he wants us to be. And that's always toward him.

When I see people in horrible predicaments and

tragedies, I often think to myself, *How can they possibly hope to cope with this? If it happened to me, I would never be able to go on.* But then I have to get a grip on this. If God has allowed it, for whatever reason, and it is part of his will even before the foundation of the earth, who am I to question it? Our tendency is to gripe, *Why me, God?* But think about that. When we say, "Why me?" we're really saying to God, "Why not someone else instead of me?" Don't go there! Whether it be the result of natural causes or accidental, he knew about it, so it just couldn't have been avoided. No matter how we replay it in our minds, we could never have avoided that appointment. When I understand it that way, no matter how awful in human terms it is, if it's part of his design, then it may not be natural, but it sure is supernatural. Then and only then, when I see it in that *light*—his light—can I begin to cope with the un-copeable.

He uses all of our predicaments to escort us right back where we belong. With him! So he always has our best interests at heart. We may think we know what we need, but in reality we only know what we want. And most of the time, what I want leads me head on into trouble because I'm always looking for the next fleeting moment of ecstasy or so I think. God is not trying to deprive us of life's little pleasures. He's directing us to his red carpet where we'll find peace and protection!

He challenges us, "Go ahead and ask me for anything. Ask, seek, and knock, and I'll let you in on my life, and don't forget to thank me for that." There is where you will find peace and nothing less. In fact, his peace will be so comforting that you won't be able to comprehend it. Even though you didn't get what you thought you needed, suddenly you're so content and can't understand why. He has a way of transcending our problems and renewing our focus. Instead of zoning in on the things we can't control, we're zoned into his presence which is perfect contentment even in the midst of tough times. So, just like a disciplined performer or athlete, *get in the zone!*

Let God call the plays and just study your playbook. I know that you have big plans for your life. So do I, but he has even bigger and better plans for our entire lives that include him in this zone and in the forever one. What, me worry? Worry never accomplished a thing except to wear me down physically, emotionally, and spiritually. Just *relax* and get in the red zone!

> "For I know the plans I have for you," declares the LORD, "plans to prosper you and not to harm you, plans to give you a hope and a future."
>
> Jeremiah 29:11

29. THE AGONY OF VICTORY AND THE THRILL OF DEFEAT!

> Sorrow is better than laughter, because a sad face is good for the heart.
>
> Ecclesiastes 7:3

Hey, that's not right. Did the typesetter twist those words around? Isn't it supposed to be "The Thrill of Victory and the Agony of Defeat"? According to popular opinion, this title is backwards but not by God's standards. No doubt about it, we do glow in our victories but let me let you in on one of life's little secrets. *We grow in defeat!* Would you rather glory for a season or grow for an eternity? That's why King Solomon, the wisest man who ever lived except for Christ, said "Sorrow is better than laughter." We'll address that in a second.

A prominent sports figure once said something to the likes of "Winning isn't everything; it's the *only* thing." Why do we place so much importance on winning? In the sports world, coming in second is simply not good enough and more than enough reason to be fired from a job as a coach or manager. No longer is the game a diversion or pleasure but instead a high pressure competition to getting the edge and bragging rights for being number one.

Worse than all of that, it's a business that drives everything about it. So they coin a phrase like "the thrill of victory and the agony of defeat." But paradoxically speaking, it's better to lose than to win. And here's why: 'cause winning puffs us up, and losing builds our character. Winning gets us all impressed with ourselves and more times than not, we get all proud and arrogant. Losing, on the other hand, may deal us a blow, but that has a way of humbling us, causing us to try harder, persevere, and maybe even ask for and depend on God's help.

We start to enjoy what we have while we have it, but when adversity strikes, and it does, it reminds us that life is short. Adversity teaches us to live wisely and that refines our character. That's the immeasurable value in suffering and sorrow. It has a refining influence on us. The world despises that, but we can learn to see it as a refining fire. Just like fire purifies fine gold and removes all the ugly residue, disappointment and failure in the long run do a real refining number on our countenance.

That's why Solomon could say that sorrow is better than laughter. He literally had it all and experienced life's best. It just made him miserable because more was never enough, and he finally labeled all of life's excess as meaningless. So he says a sad face is good for the heart. It's far better for our countenance. It makes us appreciate whatever God gives us as enough and we trust him to supply us with all that we need. We learn to value life as a gift from him for the purpose of serving him by sharing what we have with others. Then we will be flooded with his peace of mind because he gives us a new heart of humility and fulfillment. So don't sweat it if you lose the game. You're on your way to winning the war. Instead of a big head, you get a bigger heart!

For where your treasure is, there your heart will be also.

Luke 12:34

30. I DARE YOU!

"Bring the whole tithe into the storehouse, that there may be food in my house. *Test me* in this," says the LORD Almighty, "and see if I will not throw open the floodgates of heaven and pour out so much blessing that you will not have room enough for it."

Malachi 3:10

Did anyone ever dare you to do something? I recall as a kid we were always daring one another to attempt outlandish things. Dares kinda bring out the spunk in us. Dares spur us on sometimes to try stuff we normally would never attempt. Just to prove someone wrong, we'll often take a risk and lay it all on the line.

In the above verse, God is daring us. He's daring us to *trust him* in *everything!* Here the Prophet Malachi is accusing the children of Israel of robbing God of his due. In the Old Testament God demanded that his children bring a tithe or 10 percent of everything he blessed them with to his storehouse so that there could be equity for all. But the Israelites were holding back and bringing less or even the inferior from the excess of what God gave them. Malachi said they were robbing God of what he deserved and belonged to him. Therefore, everyone would suffer.

God commands the same of us. In this age of grace, he doesn't demand that Old Testament standard of 10 percent, which served as a benchmark to teach God's people to give something back. Now, since Christ has already come to earth as a man and paid in full for all of our acts of selfishness on Calvary's cross, he demands even more than that old tithe of 10 percent. Now he wants us to trust him with our entire lives, the whole kit and kaboodle. What he's saying now is, "Guys and gals, allow me to be Lord and Master of everything I've given you." In other words, he wants to be the Lord of our lives.

So this dare in Malachi 3:10 is for us too. Even though we are not bound by the Old Testament law of tithing, God is saying to us, "Folks, trust me with your whole life. *Just trust me!*" Did you notice that he tells them to bring the 10 percent into the storehouse so everyone could eat? Then he says, "Go ahead, I dare you to do it. Just do it and see if I won't open up the floodgates of heaven and rain down so much blessings on you that you won't have enough room to store it." That is some extravagant dare.

I love what Proverbs 16:15 says: "When a king's face

brightens, it means life; his favor is like a rain cloud in spring." Jesus is our King of kings and Lord of lords. And when we make him that and trust him with everything, even our finances, he will literally pour down his blessings on us like a rain cloud. But that requires making him the Lord of all of our lives. Dr. Stephen Olford once said, "He's either Lord of all or he's not Lord at all." We have to trust him with everything. No more being a control freak and trying to run our own lives and everyone else's around us. *We* have to submit to his lordship and let him call the plays. I really believe that control freaks freak out God.

Another great proverb is Proverbs 18:16. That says: "A gift opens the way for the giver and ushers him into the presence of the great." Our gifts to others open the door for God to bless us and lead us into his presence. His red carpet is rolling out again for us. It really is better to give than to receive because everyone wins. The recipient does, but God blesses the donor in a special way with his very presence. These spiritual blessings far outweigh any others in the long run.

The whole thing boils down to a matter of *trust*. Who are we trusting with our lives? Are we trusting us? With whatever management skills you may think you have, can you really control your destiny? Or are you trusting other men and women? Maybe your stockbroker or physician or lawyer or whoever. Don't make the mistake of trusting in mere men. They'll eventually disappoint you. Take God up on that dare. Go ahead and do it and trust everything you have with him.

The Prophet Jeremiah tells us that the Lord himself says, "Cursed is the *one* who trusts in *man,* who depends on *flesh* for his strength and whose heart turns away from the LORD" (Jeremiah 17:5). Jeremiah goes on to warn us that if we trust in mere man, we'll be like a bush in a desert. We'll dry up! What is interesting here is that those three different words in italics are each one a different word for man in the original Hebrew language. God's hammering the point home here. He is simply and emphatically warning us. Don't trust in anyone but him! Are you ready to take him up on his dare now? I dare you to!

> But blessed is the man who trusts in the LORD, whose confidence is in him. He will be like a tree planted by the water that sends out its roots by the stream. It does not fear when heat comes; its leaves are always green. It has no worries in a year of drought and never fails to bear fruit.
>
> Jeremiah 17:7–8

31. YOU'VE GOT MAIL!

It is right for me to feel this way about all of you, since I have you in my heart; for whether I am in chains or defending and confirming the Gospel, all of you share in God's grace with me. God can testify how I long for all of you with the *affection of Christ Jesus.*

Philippians 1:7–8

And this is my prayer: that your love may abound more and more in knowledge and depth of insight, so that you may be able to discern what is best and may be pure and blameless until the day of Christ, filled with the fruit of righteousness that comes through Jesus Christ—to the glory and praise of God.

Philippians 1:10–11

I'm closing this book with these verses from Philippians and an actual e-mail that I, a die-hard alum of Syracuse, sent to very dear friends, one a Pitt alum, during the Big East Basketball Tournament of 2006 in New York City.[4]

Dear Jeri and Vincent,

We also had a wonderful night. Good discussions and exchange of thoughts as always. Vincent, the Lord compelled me to put into practice what I was sharing with you. When we got home, I started watching the Villanova/Pitt game at the Garden. Pitt was walloping them unexpectedly, when suddenly one of the Pitt players accidentally slashed the Villanova star in the eye as they chased a loose ball. Instantly, the game became insignificant as they attended to the injured player who was in excruciating pain. He was carried off in a stretcher and ambulance to a New York City hospital.

They reported that his eyeball actually came out and was retrieved and put back in. I am not a rooter of Villanova or know about their star but remembered our discussion last night, about how Paul was so burdened and longed to pray for the Philippians from *the affection and inward parts* of Christ (Phil. 1:8). I said, "*Okay,* Christ, I know that you love this guy and now I need your affection for him to be mine too, so pray for me to intercede for him now from *your* inward parts." I found myself tossing and turning all night and lifting this guy and his family up.

They all had come to the Garden to see a championship basketball tournament and suddenly this family, parents and grandparents, found themselves in a New York hospital playing the waiting game. God gave me his compassion, and I prayed a lot last night only to find out this morning that it was not nearly as severe as initially diagnosed but a soft tissue injury and his sight returned at the hospital. They expect him to play next week in the Big Dance. Thank you, God!

So when we pray with God's affection, not ours, our prayers are effective. Praise God again for *his* affection. Needless to say, Pitt went on to win and will face the 9th seed tonight (Syracuse) for the Big East Championship. It's the first time a 9 and a 6 seed square off in this tournament, and the winner, whichever, will also be the first team that had to win 4 games in a row to win this tournament. Syracuse upset Georgetown by 1 point miraculously as we were having dinner.

So that's what prayer is all about. It's about Christ handing off his affection and inward intimacy for others to us. As I read this morning's papers, learning of Syracuse's victory, I was amazed again but I guess we of little faith shouldn't really be. Let's pray for our church and each other in that way, with the affection from the inward parts of Christ!

Love to you both and thanks again,
Bob and Marian

The grace of the LORD Jesus be with God's people. Amen.

Revelation 22:21

FINAL THOUGHTS! IF ...

If you've read the 31st chapter and are up to this point then I applaud your stick-to-a-tive-ness. I've tried to illustrate a few verses from God's word that have touched my life and I hope they've touched yours. What about your life? How do you feel about it now? I asked that question at the onset of this little journey. Are you just struggling to get up each day, going about your chores and job, collecting more stuff, letting TV and the latest electronics occupy you, and then starting all over again tomorrow?

Well, you are important and crucial to yourself, your family, your friends and colleagues, and also to your nation. The few verses that I highlighted are for you. God speaks to us personally in his word because we are important to him and we can make a difference. His word is conditional, and the consequences to it are serious to us personally and as a nation. Whatever is our cause, there will be our effect. His words will have an effect on us one way or the other. If you have embraced him and his instruction to you, you are privileged to be a part of his solution for you and your country. It's not about being influenced by some politicians and their rhetoric to get elected and govern but about trusting the promises of the Creator of you and the universe. There's an interesting Hebrew idiom in Psalm 62:11. In this psalm of David, David is saying, "One thing God has spoken, two things have I heard: that you, O God, are strong, and that you, O LORD are loving. Surely you will reward *each person* according to what he has done." When God uses this one-two repetitive punch kind of speaking in his language, he employs this repetition so we will *get it!* David is saying here, one thing: God has spoken, and two things: I heard him, I got it, it has sunk into my soul. I didn't just hear, I really listened—*I got it!*

Of all the verses that I've highlighted, one stands out to me as God's loud and clear mandate for solving the individual and global problems that we all face today. I alluded to it in chapter 15, and I'm compelled to wrap up with it here, and hopefully it will be a fresh beginning for you. Of all the verses in the Bible, here's the one that is shouting out to you and me today. Here's the answer we've all been looking for as the only genuine solution to our personal struggle with life and our world's struggle for peace. It's loud, it's clear, and it's not only pure 'n simple, it's plain 'n simple 'cause it's from God's heart to ours.

Check out 2 Chronicles 7:14 one more time and

let it sink into your soul. Don't just read it casually, but I implore you to *get it!*

After a careful meditation, can you say, "*I got it*"? Your whole world can change! It's conditional, it's cause and effect, and I believe it's the only solution to your problem and mine. If we would only wrap our souls around it and *get it! If, if, if*...here's God's mandate to us:

> *If* my people, who are called by my name, will humble themselves and pray and seek my face and turn from their wicked ways *then* will I hear from heaven and will forgive their sin and will heal their land. 2 Chronicles 7:14

There it is in plain 'n simple and pure 'n simple language. If *my* people! If you still haven't embraced him and trusted in his son, he's not addressing you here, he says, "if my people"...so he's summoning only those who belong to him by faith. He's instructing believers only here! If you do believe in him, then he is talking to you because he's called you by his name and you have heard him. Then he gives his marching orders. (1) Humble yourselves or simply come to terms with yourself. Admit your weakness and your desire to sin and ask him to fix you. Allow him to be your solution. That's the humility he wants. (2) Pray and just talk to him about you and about everything and everyone in your life that desperately needs his intervention. He's your only hope. (3) Seek his face and only his. No politician, leader, or shrink can fix you or this world. Seek means a serious encounter with him, a serious one on one relationship. Seek his face alone to do the fixing. (4) Turn from your wicked ways! You may say, "Hey, I'm not wicked, I don't do horrible things." You most likely do not, but when God uses the term "wicked," he's referring to those who don't trust in him. That's what he means by wicked. We haven't placed our trust and our lives under his control. He's simply asking for us to obey him by just trusting in his provision for our lives. His son paid our debt in full and wants to set us free. All who dwell in the deepest sin—Jesus will save if they'll just admit that to him and receive his forgiveness. There's no sin too deep for God's grace to erase.

That's it! Just embrace those four things, and he says, "*Then* will I hear from heaven and forgive their sin." Notice that he refers to our sin in the singular. That's because the overriding sin and only sin is the sin of unbelief. All the other sins spring from that! Believe in him and he will forgive everything and heal everything including our hearts and our land. That is the only hope for you and me and for our land. It's from God's mouth to our hearts. That's the verse of the hour. Did you get it? Has it sunk in? Oh, if we would only get it and get it now before our time runs out! It sounds so simple 'cause it is! It's nothing but the truth from a pure God who cares and paid heavily to cure our pain. Let him do it. He really wants to do that for *you!* He's been offering us escapades to the promised land since the beginning of time. When God parted the Red Sea, he delivered the children of Israel from their dreadful plight against the Pharaoh of Egypt by rolling out a carpet of dry land for them to pass through. And when the Angel of Death threatened to kill their firstborn male children, God instructed them to sprinkle the blood of a slain male lamb on their doorframes. Upon seeing the blood, he'd pass over their homes. Then the ultimate red carpet was unfurled on that cross of Calvary over 2000 years ago, where Jesus freely let his precious blood spill into a flowing carpet river to freedom for us.

His red carpet is still on a roll for you and me in the person of Christ. His resurrection offers us our final red carpet ride. Christ wants to personally take us by the hand and guide us as we step out on his pathway to paradise. Step out now without any reservations!

If *my* people, who are called by my name, will humble themselves and pray and seek my face and turn from their wicked ways, then will I hear from heaven and will forgive their sin and will heal their land. 2 Chronicles 7:14

ENDNOTES

1 The Highway of Holiness, The Hallmark of Honesty and The Hope of Heaven designations are from *C.S. Lewis & Francis Schaeffer* by Scott R. Burson and Jerry L. Walls.

2 Some of the concepts of this essay attributed to *Secret of the Universe* by Nathan R. Wood.

3 I am greatly indebted to David Roper and his book *Out of the Ordinary* for some of the ideas in this essay.

4 I am deeply grateful to Bill Freemen for his daily devotional *The Supplied Life*, which has inspired some of the spiritual truths in this book.